Franklin Delano Roosevelt

World War II President

By Dusk Glenn

Children's Press®

An Imprint of Scholastic Inc.

Content Consultant
Cynthia M. Koch, Ph.D.
Director of History Programming, The Franklin Delano Roosevelt Foundation at Adams House, Harvard University

Thank you to Jevon Bolden for her insights into African American history and culture.

Library of Congress Catalog-in-Publication Data
Names: Glenn, Dusk, author.
Title: Franklin Delano Roosevelt: World War II president/Dusk Glenn.
Description: New York: Children's Press, an imprint of Scholastic Inc., 2021. | Series: Presidential biographies | Includes index.
| Audience: Ages 7-9. | Audience: Grades 2-3. | Summary: "Book introduces the reader to Franklin Delano Roosevelt and his
life."—Provided by publisher.
Identifiers: LCCN 2020002637 | ISBN 9780531130971 (library binding) | ISBN 9780531130698 (paperback)
Subjects: LCSH: Roosevelt, Franklin D. (Franklin Delano), 1882-1945—Juvenile literature. | Presidents—United States—Biography—
Juvenile literature. | World War, 1939-1945—Juvenile literature. | Depressions—1929—United States—Juvenile literature. | United
States—History—1933-1945—Juvenile literature.
Classification: LCC E807 .G58 2021 | DDC 973.917092 [B]—dc23
LC record available at https://lccn.loc.gov/2020002637

Initial prototype design by Anna Tunick Tabachnik
Produced by Spooky Cheetah Press
Design by Kimberly Shake

Printed in North Mankato, MN, USA 113

SCHOLASTIC, CHILDREN'S PRESS, PRESIDENTIAL BIOGRAPHIES™, and associated logos
are trademarks and/or registered trademarks of Scholastic Inc.

1 2 3 4 5 6 7 8 9 10 R 30 29 28 27 26 25 24 23 22 21

Scholastic Inc., 557 Broadway, New York, NY 10012.

Photos ©: cover, spine: Stock Montage/Getty Images; back cover: Everett Collection/Shutterstock; 4 and throughout, 5, 6, 7,
8, 9: FDR Presidential Library & Museum; 10: World History Archive/age fotostock; 11: Thomas D. Mcavoy/The LIFE Picture
Collection/Getty Images; 13: Everett Collection/age fotostock; 14: Everett Collection/Shutterstock; 15: Blank Archives/Getty
Images; 16: Bettmann/Getty Images; 18: Carol M. Highsmith/Library of Congress; 19: Hulton Archive/Getty Images; 21: Keystone/
Getty Images; 22: U.S National Archives/Naval History and Heritage Command; 23: Bettmann/Getty Images; 24: Popperfoto/
Getty Images; 26: Library of Congress; 27: Ed Clark/The LIFE Picture Collection/Getty Images; 28: Marjory Collins/Library of
Congress; 29 top: NPS/DCPreservation.org; 29 bottom: Adam W. Louie/Flickr; 30 top left, bottom left: AP Images; 30 top
right: World History Archive/age fotostock; 30 bottom center: Oscar White/Corbis/VCG/Getty Images; 30 bottom right: FDR
Presidential Library & Museum; 31 top left: Universal History Archive/Getty Images; 31 top center: U.S National Archives/Naval
History and Heritage Command; 31 bottom left: Harris & Ewing/Library of Congress; 31 bottom right: Ed Clark/The LIFE Picture
Collection/Getty Images.

All other photos © Shutterstock.

SOURCE NOTES: Page 10: Harry L. Watson and Jane Dailey, *Building the American Republic*,
vol. 2: *A Narrative History from 1877* (Chicago: University of Chicago Press, 2016), p. 156, https://
www.bibliopen.org/p/bopen/9780226300658; page 14: Franklin D. Roosevelt's First Inaugural
Address, March 4, 1933, First Carbon Files, Speeches of President Franklin D. Roosevelt, 1933–
1945, Franklin D. Roosevelt Presidential Library, https://www.archives.gov/education/lessons/
fdr-inaugural; page 15: Franklin Roosevelt, Acceptance Speech, Democratic National Convention,
July 2, 1932, Series 1, Master Speech File, 1898–1945, Box 9, http://www.fdrlibrary.marist.edu/_
resources/images/msf/msf00494

COVER: A portrait of FDR during his first term as president.

Table of Contents

CHAPTER 1

Meet Franklin Delano Roosevelt

Franklin Delano Roosevelt, known as FDR, was the 32nd president of the United States. He was elected during a very scary time in our nation's history. Many Americans were struggling with poverty and homelessness.

FDR also led the country during World War II. Through those years, Americans relied on his strong, calm guidance. FDR is the only U.S. president to be elected four times. He achieved all that despite having had a disease called polio, which left him with a **disability**. FDR never gave up!

The effects of FDR's polio caused him to often need a wheelchair. Photos of him sitting in it are very rare.

FDR had a black Scottish terrier named Fala. Fala was the president's constant companion, and the most famous of his many dogs.

This photo of FDR was taken when he was about 14 years old.

As a young man, FDR enjoyed swimming, sailing, and riding horses.

6

A Long Struggle

Franklin was born on January 30, 1882, to a wealthy New York family. He was a distant relative of President Teddy Roosevelt, one of his childhood heroes. When FDR was 23, he married Teddy's niece Eleanor. They had six children. FDR started a promising political career as a New York state senator in 1910. But on August 11, 1921, FDR awoke to find that his legs were weak and hurt a lot. Soon, polio would cause part of his body to become **paralyzed**.

People thought FDR had no future in politics. But he persisted. Leg braces helped him stand. He learned to walk with crutches or canes.

FDR swam whenever he could to improve his strength.

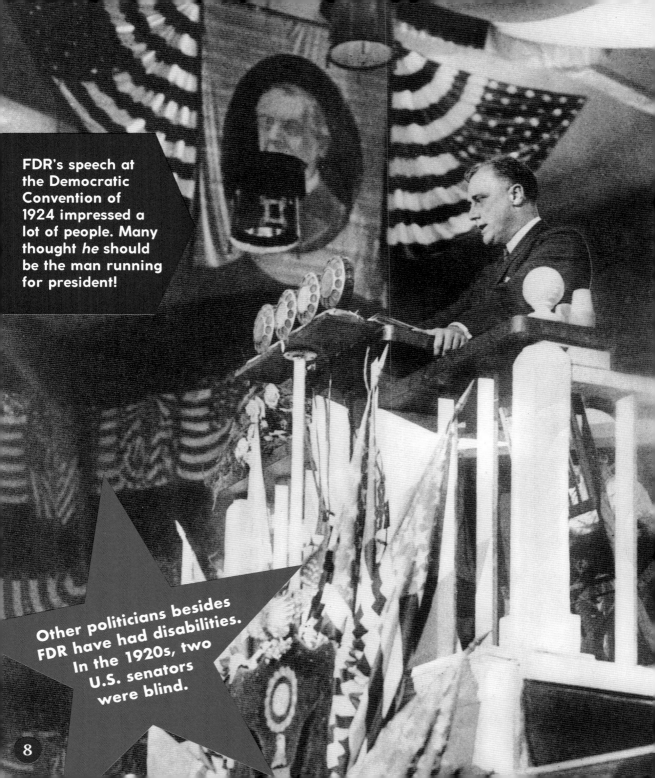

FDR's speech at the Democratic Convention of 1924 impressed a lot of people. Many thought *he* should be the man running for president!

Other politicians besides FDR have had disabilities. In the 1920s, two U.S. senators were blind.

First Steps

On June 26, 1924, FDR waited to take the stage at the Democratic National Convention. He gripped hard the arm of his son, who held FDR steady. Roosevelt was there to support another man for president.

Roosevelt crossed the platform on his crutches. To do that, he threw one leg forward at a time and used his arms to pull himself along. FDR was in pain, and he was afraid he would fall. Eight thousand people watched him silently.

When Roosevelt finally reached the speaking stand, he thrust up his chin and grinned. The audience cheered for three minutes.

FDR's son James (right) was often nearby to lend his father support.

During the Great Depresssion, unemployed men lined up to receive free soup, coffee, and doughnuts at soup kitchens across New York.

FREE SOUP
&

"We are going to make a country in which no one is left out."
—Franklin D. Roosevelt, 1933

Facing a New Crisis

In 1928, FDR was elected governor of New York State. Almost exactly a year later, in October 1929, a huge **economic** disaster occurred. It was the beginning of the Great Depression. Nearly one out of every four workers would be without a job. People would lose their life savings as banks went out of business. Many children would go hungry.

Roosevelt led New York to become the first state to offer aid to its citizens. The state hired people who needed jobs. The state government also provided food, clothing, medical aid, and other help to people in need.

FDR often spoke to Americans over the radio. His talks became known as "fireside chats."

11

CHAPTER 2

A New Deal

Meanwhile, the Depression continued to grow worse. Millions of people were hungry, homeless, or out of work. That included many **veterans**. In 1932, they went to Washington to ask for help from President Herbert Hoover. They set up camps in the city. The demonstrators came to be known as the Bonus Army.

Hoover didn't think it was the job of the federal government to help people in need. He had soldiers destroy the Bonus Army's camps and send them away.

Roosevelt received help every day because he had disabilities. He saw that other Americans needed help now, too. Roosevelt was angered by President Hoover's actions.

Many veterans in the march stayed in shacks made of packing crates, cardboard boxes, or newspapers. Shack towns such as these were called "Hoovervilles."

Members of the Bonus Army crowded the steps of the Capitol in Washington, D.C.

13

FDR's car was modified so he could drive it using hand controls.

"The only thing we have to fear is fear itself."
—Franklin D. Roosevelt, March 4, 1933

On the Edge

Roosevelt was ready to take direct action. In 1932, he ran for president. He said, "I pledge you, I pledge myself, to a new deal for the American people."

On November 8, 1932, FDR was elected president. But he didn't take office until March 1933. By that time, the United States appeared to be on the edge of disaster.

FDR needed to know what was happening around the country. But his disability made it hard for him to visit certain places. He sent Eleanor and others to study the nation's problems. Roosevelt used their reports to make decisions.

FDR's supporters wore pins like this one.

In May 1933, Eleanor visited with 1,500 veterans at this Bonus Army camp.

Eleanor Roosevelt took an active part in her husband's efforts to fight the Great Depression. By doing so, she transformed the role of First Lady.

A Helping Hand

Roosevelt's first 100 days as president were busy! He started working on his New Deal programs right away. FDR tried to get relief to people who were jobless and those who were hungry. One program he created was the Civilian Conservation Corps (CCC). Young men in the CCC planted trees, built roads, and improved public lands. They were required to send part of their pay to their families at home. FDR also created a program to help farmers keep their land. These programs alone could not end the Depression. But they could help the people who were suffering.

Veterans marched to Washington again. This time, FDR promised them jobs. Eleanor also visited the veterans. They sang songs together and shared stories.

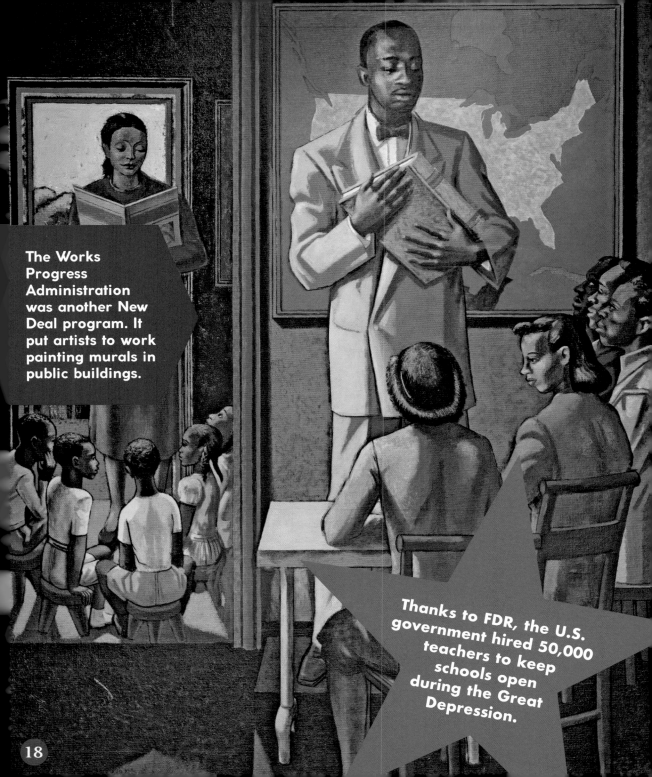

The Works Progress Administration was another New Deal program. It put artists to work painting murals in public buildings.

Thanks to FDR, the U.S. government hired 50,000 teachers to keep schools open during the Great Depression.

Growing Powers

In addition to providing relief, FDR's New Deal programs helped prevent future troubles. He made it against the law to force young children to work in dangerous conditions. He also started the Social Security program. That made sure that older people who could no longer work would have money to live.

FDR was reelected in 1936. As his second **term** came to a close, war loomed on the horizon. FDR decided to run for a third term. That had never happened before. But many Americans were afraid to make a change. They trusted FDR and wanted him to continue as president.

FDR's lifelong stamp-collecting hobby helped him relax.

CHAPTER 3

The World at War

By 1939, World War II had begun. Britain and France were fighting Nazi Germany, Italy, and Japan. Later, Britain, France, and the Soviet Union, known as the Allies, received help from other nations.

FDR had been elected to his third term as president in 1940. The United States had stayed out of the war. The American people did not want to fight. But FDR knew he had to help the Allies. He created the Lend-Lease Act. Britain was able to borrow military supplies and pay back the United States after the war. The Lend-Lease Act helped the Allies, but it also helped the United States. People were put to work creating military supplies.

In August 1941, FDR met with British Prime Minister Winston Churchill (right) to discuss their goals for the war.

By the end of World War II, the United States had provided about $50 billion in aid to more than 30 countries.

The USS *West Virginia* was one of four battleships sunk in the attack on Pearl Harbor.

More than 2,400 Americans were killed in the attack on Pearl Harbor.

Attacked!

On December 7, 1941, everything changed for the United States. The Japanese military attacked Pearl Harbor in Hawaii. The U.S. Navy's Pacific Fleet was posted there. Hundreds of U.S. planes and ships were destroyed. Thousands of Americans lost their lives.

FDR was staggered by the navy's losses. But he had to remain strong. He and Eleanor gave speeches, promising that the United States would defend itself. Thousands of Americans volunteered to join the fight. More jobs were created as training camps were built around the country, and more military supplies were manufactured. The United States had officially entered the war.

A report of the Japanese attack appeared in the December 8 edition of the *New York Times.*

Soldiers watched as Japanese Americans boarded trains bound for the prison camps.

The last Japanese prison camp was closed in March 1946.

Unequal Treatment

Sadly, **discrimination** has always existed in our country. The World War II era was no different. Black civil rights leaders worked with FDR. They tried to get better treatment for African Americans. In 1941, FDR created a program. It helped prevent discrimination in government jobs, including the military. The government didn't do as well in other areas.

After the attack on Pearl Harbor, the U.S. government worried that Japanese Americans might side with the enemy. Ten weeks after the attack, FDR signed an order. More than 100,000 Americans of Japanese descent were sent to prison camps. They had not been found guilty of plotting against the United States. Yet they were forced to leave their homes, jobs, and businesses. They lived as prisoners.

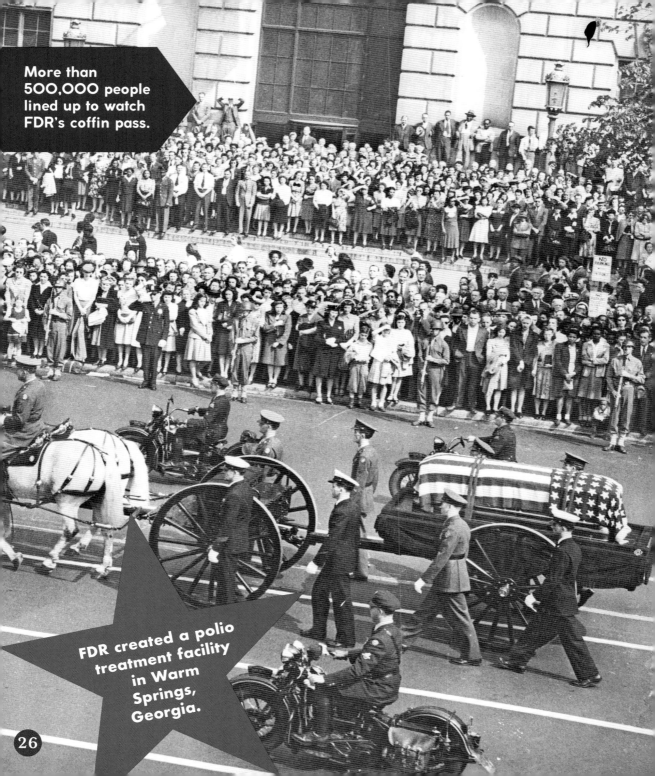

More than 500,000 people lined up to watch FDR's coffin pass.

FDR created a polio treatment facility in Warm Springs, Georgia.

Looking to the Future

Roosevelt was elected to his fourth term in 1944. The war was nearing an end—and FDR was planning for the future. He proposed an international peacekeeping group called the United Nations. He also backed the G.I. Bill, which helped veterans after the war.

But FDR would never see the future he helped shape. He died on April 12, 1945, in Warm Springs, Georgia. The war ended just four months later.

FDR pulled the United States out of the Great Depression. He led the country through the world's greatest war. Though Roosevelt was not perfect, he worked hard to make life better for many everyday Americans.

Navy Chief Petty Officer Graham Jackson played as FDR's body was taken from Warm Springs.

Housing for Americans in Need

The U.S. government built housing for Americans in need during the 1930s and 1940s. As in the rest of the country, white people and people of color were kept apart.

That practice is called segregation. One of the developments that was built for white people was in Greenbelt, Maryland. Children there played in grassy parks and playgrounds. They had a swimming pool. Underpasses went below the roads so kids could walk safely to school.

◄ Outside the movie theater at Greenbelt in the 1940s

The housing development at Langston Terrace, past (top) and present (bottom)

Langston Terrace was an apartment complex in Washington, D.C., that was built for African American families. There, children climbed on concrete animal sculptures in a wide courtyard. There were no grassy parks or swimming pools. As is often the case with segregation, the housing for Black families was not equal to the housing for white families. It was worse. Segregation was outlawed in the United States in 1964. But it would be many decades before people of color were given the same opportunities as white people in this country.

29

American History

1883
The Brooklyn Bridge is opened in New York.

1901
On September 14, Theodore Roosevelt takes over as president of the United States after President McKinley is assassinated. Roosevelt is elected on his own in 1904.

1929
The biggest economic downturn in history, known as the Great Depression, begins in October.

| 1882 | 1883 | 1901 | 1905 | 1921 | 1929 |

FDR's Life

1882
FDR is born in New York on January 30.

1905
On March 17, FDR marries Eleanor Roosevelt.

1921
In August, FDR becomes disabled after contracting polio.

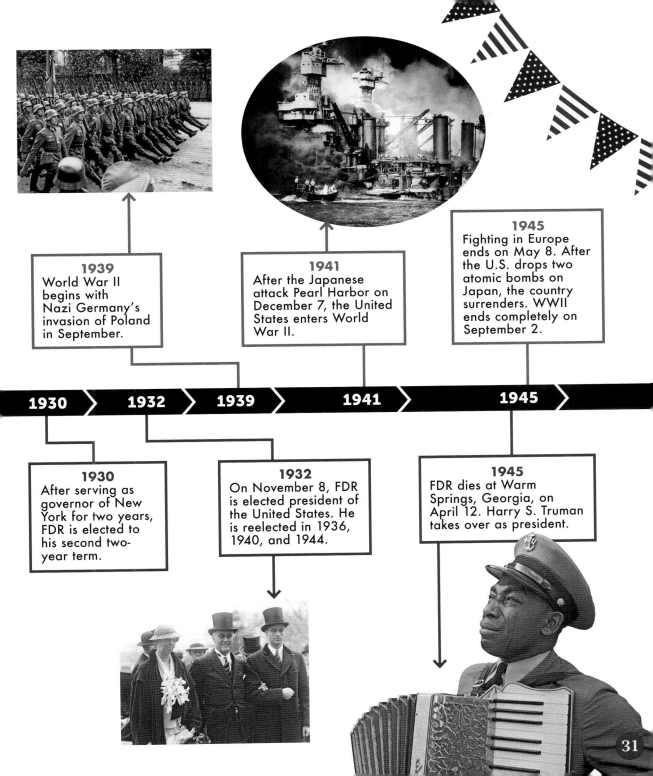

1939
World War II begins with Nazi Germany's invasion of Poland in September.

1941
After the Japanese attack Pearl Harbor on December 7, the United States enters World War II.

1945
Fighting in Europe ends on May 8. After the U.S. drops two atomic bombs on Japan, the country surrenders. WWII ends completely on September 2.

| 1930 | 1932 | 1939 | 1941 | 1945 |

1930
After serving as governor of New York for two years, FDR is elected to his second two-year term.

1932
On November 8, FDR is elected president of the United States. He is reelected in 1936, 1940, and 1944.

1945
FDR dies at Warm Springs, Georgia, on April 12. Harry S. Truman takes over as president.

GLOSSARY

disability (dis-uh-BIL-i-tee): something that prevents someone from being able to move easily, or from being able to act or think in ways typically expected of a person

discrimination (dis-krim-i-NAY-shuhn): prejudice or unfair behavior to others based on differences in such things as age, race, or gender

economic (ek-uh-NAH-mik): of or having to do with the system of buying, selling, making things, and managing money in a place

paralyzed (PAR-uh-lized): unable to move or feel a part of the body

term (TURM): a definite or limited amount of time

veterans (VET-ur-uhnz): people who have served in the armed forces, especially during a war

INDEX

ABOUT THE AUTHOR

Dusk Glenn is the author of *The Triangular Trade: What Did Enslaved Africans Experience?* A former journalist, Glenn is a history writer and an avid reader of books for young people. Visit duskglenn.com to learn more.